# I CAN'T KEEP MY OWN SECRETS

## SIX-WORD MEMOIRS
### BY TEENS FAMOUS + OBSCURE

**FROM SMITH MAGAZINE**

EDITED BY RACHEL FERSHLEISER AND LARRY SMITH

HARPER TEEN
*An Imprint of HarperCollinsPublishers*

HarperTeen is an imprint of HarperCollins Publishers.

www.harperteen.com
Submit your six-word memoir at www.smithteens.com.

Library of Congress Cataloging-in-Publication Data
I can't keep my own secrets : six-word memoirs by teens famous & obscure :
from Smith magazine / edited by Rachel Fershleiser & Larry Smith. — 1st ed.
        p.     cm.
    "This is a book with over 600 authors (all aged thirteen to nineteen) and
600 characters (all real, as far as we know) and 600 stories (which can be read
in any order). What every story has in common is that each was written about
the author's own life, and that each is the exact same length: six words."
    ISBN 978-0-06-172684-2
    1. Autobiographies.   2. Teenagers' writings.   I. Fershleiser, Rachel.
II. Smith, Larry, 1968–   III. Smith magazine.
CT107.I25   2009                              2009014584
808'.06692—dc22                                   CIP
                                                   AC

Typography by Sasha Illlingworth
    10   11   12   13      CG/CW      10   9   8   7   6   5   4
❖
First Edition

## This is the story of six. . . .

Most memoirs are books written by one person and are meant to be read from start to finish. There's one overall story with a beginning, middle, and end, plus some characters you get to know pretty well.

This is not one of those books.

This is a book with over 600 authors (all aged thirteen to nineteen) and 600 characters (all real, as far as we know) and 600 stories (which can be read in any order). What every story has in common is that each was written about the author's own life, and that each is the exact same length: six words.

The idea of telling an entire story in half a dozen words dates back to Ernest Hemingway. Legend has it that this great American writer was once challenged to write a whole novel in just six words. He came back with "For sale: baby shoes, never worn." Since then, writers have been exploring the six-word story in many shapes and forms. Our idea was to ask readers for their six-word memoir—there's no topic you're a bigger expert on than yourself.

Last year, we published *Not Quite What I Was Planning: Six-Word Memoirs by Writers Famous & Obscure*, a collection of hundreds of slices of life that was hugely popular. The book sparked people of all ages around the world to create their own memoirs. Teachers from kindergarten to graduate school used them as exercises in classrooms, and ministers and rabbis brought them into sermons. People put on six-word-inspired plays, wrote six-word songs, and filmed their own YouTube videos. In a high school in south Texas, students made paintings and sculptures to illustrate their six-word memoirs and debuted the show in a gallery.

Back at SMITH Magazine, we couldn't wait to hear more. We challenged teens to continue the trend by telling the story of your lives in just six words, and you blew us away. You revealed secrets about your families ("Falling apart because Dad's behind bars."), your hearts ("In love with best friend's boyfriend."), and the tough road life can lead you down ("Seventeen, pregnant. He's off to Iraq."). You offered up your big dreams ("I'm poor. I'm going to Harvard.") and guiding philosophies ("Life lessons found in *Scrubs* episodes."). You told us about battles with disease ("Fifteen and my mom has cancer."), food ("Bulimia was only cramping my style."), and technology ("According to Facebook, we broke up."). Many of you are still trying to figure out the questionable calls your parents made ("I was named after a store.").

When we were teens, our secrets filled journals stuffed under mattresses; you share your stories with one another and the world. On your blogs, your MySpace and Facebook pages, and at places like PostSecret and SMITHteens, you're the leaders of a revolution, using personal storytelling to connect everyone.

This book contains hundreds of six-word stories, written by and for teens across America and beyond. Each word and every image came from over 600 contributors. If you're new to all this, we hope you'll read it and be inspired to write your own. Everyone has a story—what's yours?

Rachel Fershleiser and Larry Smith
April 2009, New York City
SMITH Magazine • www.smithmag.net •
www.smithteens.com

Told you I'd be published someday!
—*Kay A.*


Born in the wrong decade, man.
—*Victoria D.*


Half sister doesn't
know I'm alive.
—*Emily R. M.*


Met online; love before first sight.
—*Chris S.*

I own nine pairs of Converse.

—*Maddie F.*


Music and God
are my constants.

—*Aubrey H.*


A roller-coaster ride of
unbelievable events.

—*Micah M.*


I'm army boots. Ready for battle.

—*Amanda L.*

Five elementary schools
and two obituaries.

—*Eunice B.*

# My name will someday be remembered.

—*Claudia R.-G.*

Born 1992. Unhappy. Adopted 2007. Happy.

—*Tabitha G.*

**Eventually, I'll make my own breakfast.**

—*Sam Z.*

Rather be alone in my room.

—*Anais V.*

You're the parent, act like one.

—*Lily M.*


Hung myself.

Sister found me.

Alive.

—*Anna-Lise M.*


**Don't believe in love.
Only science.**

—*Hannah D.*


I only tell truth in journals.

—*Rachel W.*

First I hone; then I pwn.

*—Dan G.*

**Daddy's little angel, Mom's right hand.**

*—Angelica R.*

I just want to feel infinite.

*—Phoebe G.*

# Boob exposure and salary increase unrelated.

*—Rhiannon P.*

Fears:

jellyfish,

cocaine,

stray hairs,

heartbreak.

—*Jane H.*

My mind soars on paper airplanes.

—*Bridget H.*

Money's tight; thankfully imagination is free.

—*Vanessa E.*

Teen victim of shooting:
lost leg.

—*Chris H.*

I seriously love school bean burritos.

—*Kenna J.*

Never been kissed.
Don't want to.
    —*Katherine R.*

I edit my profile, or vice-versa?
    —*Noa B.-S.*

Can't chew gum without blowing bubbles.
    —*Laura H.*

Ripped open,

sewn back up,

healing.
    —*Traci V.*

Called him, but he hung up.
                    —*Amanda B.*


## Mom just revoked my creative license.
                    —*Nur A.*


*Nada y pues nada,*
Hemingway says.
                    —*Louis E.*


`They screamed "nobody."`

`I believed them.`
                    —*Andrew C.*

Living my dream;

please send money.

—*Brittney L.*

When I jump, no one catches.

—*Brionna L.*

# I'm deaf, but she can't hear.

—*Rosemary F.*

`I like to fix broken things.`

—*Rachel T.*

Bulimia was only cramping my style.

—*Mary A.*

Found the "One," scared he'll run.
—*Ashleigh B.*

# I stopped reading between the lines.

—*Alicia F.*

I looked it up on Wikipedia.
—*Maya A.*

Wikipedia didn't know either.
Oh well.
—*Jessica Z.*

# Contemplated joining circus.

## Foolishly chose college.

—*Sally C.*

You are my sixty-second sunset.

—*Wendy K.*


Can't stop taking
pictures of myself.

—*Kacey K.*


Some hairs grew on my face.

—*Wade P.*


Only seventeen;
already using wrinkle cream.

—*Kristy M.*

Grandma's dying
while I'm out shopping.

—*Sara M.*

# Exaggeration is the spice of life.

*—Eve G.*


Stillborn baby lost, I found God.

*—Lydia S.*


# My dad has more MySpace friends.

*—Daryle J.*


**Fat camp makes fat campers fatter.**

*—Ava C.*

Never been drunk.

Never been happier.

—*Leah V.*

# I always imagine clowns without makeup.

—*Visala A.*

Intensive care stopped my self-destruction.

—*Emma P.*

God abandoned me, so I reciprocated.

—*Amy M.*

I can't look at babies anymore.

—*Evie S.*

One egg. Two girls.
Best friends.
　　　　　—*Bethany D.*


You left no note.
I'm heartbroken.
　　　　　—*Jillian T.*


Sorry,
　but I'm with the band.
　　　—*Liz M.*


Can say I beat depression,
　　　　　finally.
　　　　　—*Lizzy A.*

Aspiration: colonize Mars.
You're not invited.

—*Jordan H.*

*One Tree Hill* changed my life.

—*Ju P.*

Polaroid photographs taken
of prospective boyfriends.

—*Rachel C.*

Call me "hippie."
I. Dare. You.

—*Maggie R.*

I'd rather be eating a cheeseburger.

—*Zoe R.*

I used too much Texas Pete.
—*Abigail T.*


Spent more time reading
than living.
—*Martha G.*


I am more than just gay.
—*Alex K.*


# Wow. I lived to see eighteen.
—*Sarah M.*

```
Straight and narrow,
straight to hell.
```
                              —*Julie Z.*


**Daddy issues are all I know.**
                              —*Amanda H.*


In love with best friend's boyfriend.
                    —*Elizabeth F.*


One house; never had a home.
                    —*Jessica H.*

Hypnotism changed my life.
Go figure.

—*Rachel N.*

# I will be that cat lady.

—*Rolynda T.*

Dreams too big for this town . . .

—*Megan M.*

**I resent people who ignore grammar.**

—*Molly S.*

# I never got my Hogwarts letter.

—*Deanna H.*

I love you,
please stop drinking.

—*Kristina R.*

## You still smell like my childhood.

—*Sarah R.*

**I plan on breaking her heart.**

—*Neil C.*

First time hazy.
    Blame the booze.

—*Juliana R.*

Rejected by parents,
nowhere to go.
                    —*Marlee V.*


Current status in life equals wallflower.
                    —*Kaitlyn C.*


I'm still scared of a B-plus.
                    —*Carmel B.-S.*


They had sex and I watched.
                    —*Mike S.*

Sick of being the good child.

—*Laura K.*

Lost 130 pounds for your attention.

—*Elizabeth C.*

My art was better than me.

—*Jewels H.*

I am definitely my mother's daughter.

—*Andrea W.*

Catholic girl desperately wants her faith.

—*Emma F.*


I have curves!
I love mirrors.

—*Rebecca H.*


Live in Canada. Not an igloo.

—*Mackenna C.*


Not your average teen angst bullshit.

—*Amanda L.*

```
It is very
          very
               very
                    complicated.
```
—*Kika M.*


# I am only creative on
# MySpace.

—*Adrienne D.*


**David Bowie:**
**my drug of choice.**

—*Kelsey O.*


# I sold all my Barbie dolls.

—*Cameron V.*

Atheist.

So much for Hebrew school.

—*Zachary R.*

Pen to paper, all I need.
—*Tyra B.*


Turn around, and you're all alone.
—*Lizzi G.*


# My friends don't know:
# I believe.
—*Jessica L.*


**Turned thirteen and don't feel different.**
—*Ena S.*

Friend.

Boyfriend.

Ex-boyfriend.

Friend.

Friend's boyfriend.

*—Maura M.*

Music is love; band is drama.

—*Kendra G.*

# Refusing to be
## just another statistic.

—*Brittany G.*

I was so much happier fat.

—*Lauren H.*

Can't live without
a little insanity.

—*Sara R.*

Fifteen and my mom has cancer.

—*Demi M.*

# I live bigger than your labels.

—*Samantha N.*

Big orange couch;
miss the 90s.

—*Hannah D.*

Male humans were my childhood fear.

—*Desiree M.*

And all I wanted were doughnuts.
—*Kari D.*

# Three high schools.
# Only uniforms change.
—*Keerthana J.*

`Can't get over my dead family.`
—*Kristen C.*

PHX to PDX. Best. Move. Ever.
—*Maddie R.*

Girl meets boy. Boy is gay.

—*Kate M.*

Salinger.
Sartre.
King.
Camus.
Vonnegut.
Huxley.

—*Stephanie C.*

Eccentricity is not an exact science.

—*Melissa L.*

I am almost always missing something.

—*Nina F.*

Gave up one addiction
for another.

—*Marissa L.*

# Finally learned "weird"
# is a compliment.

—*Teagan E.*

HIV: We could have saved her.

—*Kathryn L.*

**Never shopping at
Wet Seal again.**

—*Aimee M.*

Roots are shallow, wings are broken.

—*Kelly V.*

I hate your one-word replies.

—*Trisha D.*

Dan saved my life; doesn't know.

—*Stephanie H.*

Failed driver's test. Meant to pass.

—*Samantha T.*

Not enough room in the margins.

—*Coreen G.*

Homecoming king
with a
septum ring.

—*Reid K.*

Grew up, kept my childish heart.

—*India K.*


I wish "Sir" was "Dad" instead.

—*Sarah B.*


Autistic brothers
give the best hugs.

—*Kristen C.*


Gamer girls will rule the world!

—*Shawna F.*

My status messages are about you.

—*Elissa S.*

Always end up marring my manicure . . .

—*Elisha M.*

Lost virginity to *Speed Racer* theme.

—*Raella R.*

I'm just a simple human.
Being.

—*Nic H.*

I run on the rainy days.

—*Alessandra W.*


Coming out was not the answer.

—*Alice K.*


**Best first was falling in love.**

—*Abby K.*


Braces were sucky, perfect teeth now.

—*Lola L.*

# The keys I have don't fit.

*—Alicia K.*

## Iraq doesn't need you. I do.

*—Alicia Marie S.*

I'm secretly
much older than fifteen.

*—Rachel C.*

```
A never-ending series of

marvelous misadventures.
```
*—Kirby S.*

Wake up.
Pee.
Step on scale.
—*Kia W.*


Googled what he called me.
Ouch.
—*Emily L.*


Started growing up way too early.
—*Kathryn A.*


# Follow your dreams.
# Not your parents.
—*Srishti K.*

Note to all boys: I quit.

—*Lauren A.*

History.
Math.
Study hall.
Birthing coach.
—*Laura D.*


# Wish I could color outside lines.
—*Samantha S.*


```
Ostracized as Catholic.
Exonerated as lesbian.
```
—*Kris H.*


Falling for pirates, Brits, vampires, Italians.
—*Natalie C.*

```
Family has bipolar disorder.
Me too.
```
                                   —*Katie M.*


They don't know, but we're engaged.
                                   —*Emily O.*


```
Great uncle's on the AIDS quilt.
```
                                   —*Stephanie N.*


# Defined by numbers:
# age,
# weight,
# SATs.
                         —*Jocelyn P.*

Would be a slut, given chance.

—*Laurel G.*

I have blisters on my fingers.

—*Geoff B.*

**Read *Lord of Flies*. Threw up.**

—*Jake S.*

Luck was on my side . . . luckily.

—*Alexis W.*

Dragged across country, decided to stay.

—*Lily B.*


## Natural blonde dyed black. Values intact.

—*Michelle E.*


Day: average girl.
Night: gaming addict.

—*Miranda C.*


## Live in Arkansas; parents aren't related.

—*Shane G.*

School lunches by myself were best.

—*Abby J.*

Quiet personality finds its loud daily.

—*Sam S.*

**Known as depressed.**

**Happier every day.**

—*Saskia D.*

My chemistry teacher is a hero.

—*Gabrielle R.*

I really don't mind being autistic.

—*Lisa D.*

My 10th toenail
    finally grew back.
        —*Blue L.*


**Can't find home.**
**Won't stop looking.**
        —*Kelsey G.*


Lost my virginity.
    It was fantastic.
        —*Jessica S.*


Planted a tree and
    studied magic.
        —*Leah G.*

Best friends.
Text messages.
Summer love.

—*Tiffany B.*


Okay with not going to prom.

—*Molly B.*


**They weren't my cup of soup.**

—*Elaine W.*


Got expelled. Felt like living again.

—*Alexis G.*

# I am thankful for cheap aprons.

*—Kate D.*

Met online, leaving America for him.

—*Aerith M.*

I'm looking forward to the future.

—*Paige M.*

7UP through the nose: I'm happy.

—*Ally H.*

I'm not the Katie you knew.

—*Katelyn W.*

Damn, I think it's sorta beautiful.

—*April J.*

Honor roll. No friends. "Bright future."

—*Anne Q.*

Proud lesbian,
but my girlfriend isn't.

—*Shawna C.*

Marines are stealing you from me.

—*Jasmine A.*

If not through whispers, in texts.

—*Hannah S.*

Making paper cranes, need the luck.

—*Zoe K.*


Teen version of Peter Pan syndrome.

—*Cherish R.*


```
Honestly,
I hate all my friends.
```

—*Michelle D.*


Summer camp: alone, with Sedaris anecdotes.

—*Pearl M.*

Flautist who wants to play percussion.

—*Elise C.*

Marching band has saved my life.

—*Kristin H.*

```
Stole sign warning
not to steal.
```

—*Jill D.*

High school Aspy, never really understood.

—*Mike W.*

A time machine would be nice.

—*Kelsey W.*

I still find solace in Shakespeare.

—*Kerry H.*

# He said I wasn't worth it.

—*Diana H.*

**Thought I ought,**
    **so sought,**
        **wrought.**

—*Lily G.*

Can't understand:
    math,
      life,
        time,
          you.

—*Natalia J.*

Sister of five.
Still so lonely.
—*Emily C.*

Texting in class,
lost my phone.
—*Nicole G.*

Shepherd's daughter.
Hip-hop dancer.
Wannabe assassin.
—*Ziggy D.*

# Against the odds, I got out.
—*Eva C.*

Love my daddy;
Daddy loves drugs.
—*Tristen W.*

Edward Cullen
is my fictional boyfriend.
—*Adrianna B.*

I drank sweet tea and cried.
—*Allie C.*

Called me stupid,
I'm only dyslexic.
—*Noel B.*

# I thought you said you'd call.

—Jennifer G.

```
Falling apart because
Dad's behind bars.
```

—Yumeji V.

I always liked average boys best.

—Macy B.

Inspired to sing by my grandma.

—Alysiana E.

People survive hurricanes;
Gustav's not different.

—*Adelaide E.*

Two cheerleading sisters.
I chose acting.

—*Maggie M.*

# Always listening,
# but never really heard.

—*Agnes T.*

Never met him,
but love him.

—*Grace K.*

I regret sleeping with
my teacher.

—*Jordan F.*

My psychiatrist is
the crazy one.

—*Scarlet J.*

School in NY; lover in AK.

—*Jeffrey C.*

Nerdy, obsessive, awkward. So much fun.

—*Samantha P.*

# Slowly becoming everything that I hate.

—*Julia D.*

I gave myself a new identity.

—*India R.*


People with Down's are more alive.

—*Adrienne B.*


Learned to play
piano without teacher.

—*Ana G.*


Too young to hate my brothers.

—*Tirzah P.*

**Life of faith,
world of sin.**

—*Sarah M.*

# My true colors
# are very bright!

—*Alexandria Marie A.*

"The good daughter,"

and therefore invisible.

—*Rachel B.*

## Collected shot glasses since age seven.

—*Maria T.*

Girls like giant fighting robots, too.

—*Shawna F.*


God has him. I miss him.

—*Chantelle G.*


Always forgetting
to bring an umbrella.

—*Freda D.*


My teacher ruined music for me.

—*Theresa H.*

Blessed with good mom and breasts.

—*Ashley L.*

Being scared has saved my
life.

—Stephanie D.

# He proposed.
# I'm fourteen.
# He's seventeen.

—Briana R.

Coffee and spiders.
    Won't ever end.

—Jennifer F.

# Laughed at abuser's funeral.
# Feel guilty.

—Ashley P.

# I guess this is growing up.

—*Hannah T.*

Allergic to reality;
compelled by fiction.

—*Ally O.*

`Granddad died.`
`Dad didn't tell me.`

—*Shauna J.*

# Sleeping through my alarm

# saved me.

—*Harriet T.*

# Had twins then had an abortion.

—*Brandi B.*

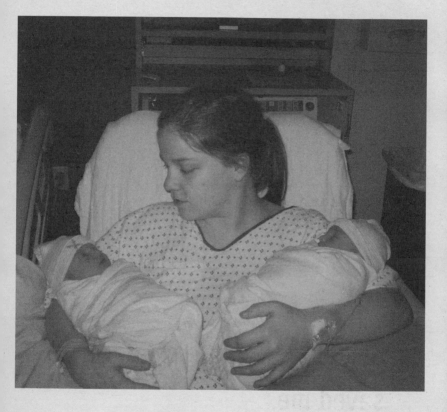

My words in purple print?
Priceless.

—*Valarie P.*

# Skinny girl in a fat body.

—*Victoria F.*

**My name is my mom's backwards.**

—*Anylec S.*

Asperger's does not define my life.

—*Mary Ellen M.*

SVA too pricey, settled for KSU.

—*Bridget E.*


Thankfully, running took over my life.

—*Marie A.*


# Gay and never dated a man.

—*David S.*


Fear: losing mom.
Faith: gaining another.

—*Cassandra F.*

Late to
school
every
single
day.

—*Mindy T.*

I'm just standing in the background.

—*Sarah B.*

# You made me stronger. Thanks, rapist.

—*Alyssa Z.*

## Born in transit; been there since.

—*Sasha F.*

Play blues guitar, it'll pan out.

—*Jace C.*

```
Chicken Soup for the Obese Soul.
```
—*Wesley T.*


I have given myself 1,131 injections.
—*Jamie S.*

You chose pot,
    I chose poetry.
—*Sara M.*


Anything
        but monotone.
I am Technicolor.
—*Nancy B.*

Born thyroidless, but God's healing me.

—*Alisha W.*

# Tried being reasonable.
# Now I'll rebel.

—*Amanda L.*

Always helping others. Never helping myself.

—*Alexandra S.*

`Black parents gave birth: white child.`

—*Amber M.*

I think I fell in love.

—*Jody V.*

Found out I had
cancer.

Damn.

—*Cornelius L.*

I told him everything.
Big mistake.

—*Lindsay B.*

A boy wizard saved my life.

—*Rebecca G.*

Family falls apart after mom dies.

—Caroline C.

Living with asthma for 18 years.

—*Ashley H.*

Never complete
without whiskey and pen.

—*Moriah C.*

Always all-county, never all-state.

—*Lena B.*

I've
    only
        been
            stable
            four
                months.

—*Lily S.*

It was an honest mistake,

really.
—*Sophie K.*


Jesus saves, my ass.
Comma justified.
—*Hali H.*


I lied: I was a virgin.
—*Abby S.*


You blog. I bottle it up.
—*Yolandra B.*

Me plus brother equals
total disaster.

—Zachary M.


The fireworks were gone by then.

—Emily V.


Been kissed once.
High school dare.

—Ebony L.


I'm only

popular

during summer camp.

—Beatrice M.

I walked on eggshells;
they cracked.

—*Katie N.*


# I know they wanted a boy.

—*Jacqulin K.*


Token Asian, fat friend.
Lovin' it.

—*Jenny S.*


"Mom, you laughing at me?"
"Yes."

—*Annie C.*

You're gone, and I'm still praying.

—*Jose D.*

I need out of Ohio. **Bad.**

—*Kate P.*

Met him once.
Changed me forever.

—*Juliah D.*

I lost more
than my innocence.

—*Angela G.*

Hair's pink to
piss you off.

—*Stephanie N.*

# Wrote a song. Not for you.

—*Ethan H.*

```
She's prettier,
but I have personality.
```
—*Keerthana J.*

## Basically, all I want is Yale.

—*Ashley S.*

```
"Good son" was really "bad son."
```
—*Kenneth O.*

The distance

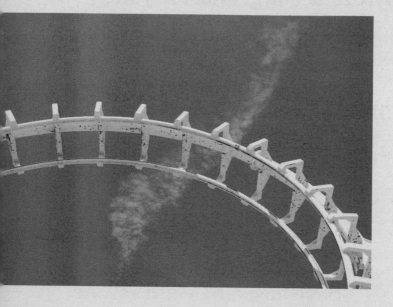

could never

break us.

*—Lindie D.*

**Still ride shopping carts down stairs.**

*—Julia F.*

**You have to earn your beers.**

*—Katie W.*

He's my blue box, cheesy romantic.

*—Lisa Marie H.*

**Lost myself for popular kids' approval.**

*—Kimberly G.*

Stepmom cheated.
I can't stand her.
—*Jocelyn M.*

# I love you.
# Stop selling weed.
—*Kat J.*

**She's 37.**
**I'm 17.**
**It's good.**
—*Phil S.*

Couldn't sing
so played the drums.
—*Rachel M.*

They say Oreo. I say raceless.

—*Loren W.*


Read the thesaurus on the toilet.

—*Dan R.*


Swerved off road, but kept driving.

—*Khalil M.*


Only born because older sister died.

—*Lyra W.*

Chose happiness
over anger and hate.
—*Samsara R.*


Because the chicken is a nonconformist.
—*Dillon W.*


Was pregnant.

Lost it.

His fault.
—*Yesenia I.*


It was love at first sight.
—*Vanessa K.*

My weird elbows make me special.

—*Julie W.*

Smoke detectors
taught me to cook.

—*Ivy V.*

The fun came before the awkward.

—*Lacey M.*

Life was complete.
    Then thunder struck.

—*Melissa D.*

The exits

were entrances

in disguise.

—*Shannon B.*

His abuse made me respect myself.

—*Lindsey E.*

I found my sister in college.

—*Natalie G.*

**Learned that sometimes friends aren't forever.**

—*Victoria L.*

Change my mind, change the world.

—*Vanessa M.*

Lost my shoes.
Found winged sandals.
—*Kily W.*

I'm still living in my past.
—*Verushka C.*

Remember your voice.
Wish I couldn't.
—*Kelsey L.*

A purring cat makes everything better.
—*Callista W.*

Family night is secretly my favorite.

—*Lindsey D.*

Too boring
to contribute
anything worthwhile . . .
　　　　　　　*—Kajhal M.*

```
Bulimic, obese.
Not what I expected.
```
　　　　　　　　*—Jasmine K.*

**That river trip forever changed me.**
　　　　　　　　　　*—Cora C.*

**Loved college until I got there.**
　　　　　　　　　*—Adrienne W.*

Waiting indefinitely for life to begin.
                                        —*Jocelyn P.*

Cheer captain and
valedictorian:
stereotype annihilator.
                                        —*Laura R.*

Fell down,
        got up,
                kept dreaming.
                                        —*Megan K.*

He's twenty, twice jailed,
                and perfect.
                                        —*Jasmin M.*

Still wishing for (ctrl+z) undo command.

—Joanna L.

I am falling with the redwoods.

—Violet H.

Destroyed brick walls
with bloody fists.

—Jared R.

You wanted
me aborted.
How sad.

—Thaise B.

Burnbook I wrote ruined my life.

—*Cassa P.*

I won't need photographs to remember.

—*Paige M.*

Nine siblings.

Two families.

One me.

—*Lynn C.*

Everything's done for that college application.

—*Elizabeth C.*

—*Stephanie M.*

Measured out my life in literature.
—*Jessica S.*


I can't keep my own secrets.
—*Catriona E.*



ADD, OCD. Sucks to be me.
—*Emily Victoria H.*


I define bisexuality.
Not vice versa.
—*Annelies D.*

Am a ballerina, still totally clumsy.

—*Emma W.*

Freshman: first love.
Sophomore: first heartbreak.

—*Rosalie A.*

Dying to smoke,
smoking to die.

—*Christina M.*

Hated every hipster.
Now I'm one.

—*Susan D.*

I enjoy black-and-white television.
> —*Cara Z.*

Jailed dad and patient mom.
**Divorced.**
> —*Carolina J.*

# I dance
## with skeletons
## from closets.
> —*Ilana S.*

Take me back to swings, fireflies.
> —*Cimara D.*

Lost a dollar; found a five.

—*Charmaine T.*

I tried to conform. It backfired.

—*Kylie N.*

Small-town girl,
    big-city dreams.

—*Sara A.*

Learned sarcasm.
    Sorry, it's outta control.

—*Kevin W.*

Queer,
  gay,
    homo,
  faggot:
just labels.
—*Callan H.*


New state,
  my past is private.
—*Katherine P.*


He said bye with YouTube links.
—*Melissa B.*


Hold my insulin, not my hand.
—*Cody S.*

Thank god I am an atheist.

—*Chelsea C.*


Monsters under bed remain,
just changed.

—*Carolyn S.*


# Seventeen, pregnant.
# He's off to Iraq.

—*Casey M.*


Maps make the journey less interesting.

—*McAllister C.*

I'll have a *True Hollywood Story*.
                              —*Eric V.*


Almost graduated and I'm scared shitless.
                              —*Chelsea U.*


Childhood fantasy: Living in a library.
                              —*Bethany B.*


Views on

          life,

                    love,

                              universe:

                                        TBA.
                              —*Charlotte T.*

Not used to smiles.
            Prefer smileys.
                        —*Caroline B.*


**Eating is harder than it looks.**
                        —*Ava C.*


# Love my dog more than Mom.
                        —*Sarah G.*


I don't know if I believe.
                        —*Abigail D.*

Experimented once.
Almost died.
Experimented twice.
—*Camila G.*


Broken.

Loved anyway.

I'm so thankful.
—*Kayla P.*


I never got to tell him. . . .
—*Vanidie S.*


Experimented once.
Almost died.
Changed forever.
—*Stephen B.*

My mom

had my boyfriend

deported.

—*Candra T.*

My heart belongs to New York.
—*Samantha M.*

# In the nest, twigs are sharp.
—*Justin M.*

`Never felt beautiful without my piercings.`
—*Jeniva Q.*

Haven't talked since. Heartbroken since February.
—*Jorge A.*

Computer ate my soul.

Yours, too.
—*Lindsey Elise S.*


Desperate to explore, yet stuck here.
—*Ruth C.*


Laughed at all the wrong moments.
—*Kierra B.*


I miss all my imaginary friends.
—*Stephanie C.*

I like taking pictures of feet.

—*Elyse B.*

I'm seventeen,

engaged,

and not pregnant.
—*Delaney P.*


Scared of God,
    curious of occult.
—*Jessica B.*


I traded my brick for straw.
—*Laney F.*


I draw my dreams in crayon.
—*Riley S.*

In Scouts eight years, still there.

—*Lance W.*

American girl infatuated with British boys.

—*Nicole M.*

```
I have accepted your

abandonment, Dad.
```

—*Anisa M.*

Came out to Mom. All better.

—*Kaitlyn S.*

We are banned
from Wal-Mart
forever.

—*Kristin S.*

**I saw it coming. Wasn't prepared.**

—*Ezabell T.*

Anything's possible
in dreams and fanfic.

—*Paige M.*

# I will be a paramedic someday.

—*Lauren B.*

Perfectionistic poets
don't make good money.

—*Emily H.*

Short trans male.
Looking for love.

—*Shae G.*

# Dying to go to boarding school.

—*Sonia B.*

**I fulfilled my
awkwardness quota today.**

—*Maggie A.*

Mixed race. What am I now?

—*Aaron B.*

# Brain too big, boobs too small.

—*Jeanie A.*

```
Heart: romantic;
head: cynic;
together: torn.
```
—*Jenny S.*

**He only knew one word: meh.**

—*Olivia G.*

I've loved her for eight years.

—*Alice L.*

Got three sisters and two dads.

—*Ella R.*

Have permit. Still can't drive away.

—*Maryssa B.*

Premature midlife crisis at age seventeen.

—*Aqila A.*

My scars:
Everybody stares.
Nobody asks.

—*Bonnie B.*

Eighteen feels like eighty.
Disability sucks.

—*Claire G.*

**Tired of waiting to be older.**

—*Nicole P.*

Parents are separated. Have two homes.

—*Autumn M.*

**Pack a day (chew, not smoke).**

—*Talia M.*

Always the friend,

never the girl.

—*Kristy D.*

Called to ministry. Can't tell anyone.

—*Christina N.*

Praying that "adulthood"
doesn't mean "amnesia."

—*Betsy O.*

```
Abused child found invincible love within.
```
—*Francine H.*

Lived vicariously.
Laughed gregariously.
Died virgin.

—*Payal S.*

Would be happier with her sister.
—*Landon O.*

I discovered myself through being Jewish.
—*Sarah D.*

Living off Advil
and peanut butter.
—*Sylvia Y.*

Another Indiana night spent at home.
—*Emili H.*

Fell in love with best friend.

—*Magie F.*

**Guitar string snapped. I kept playing.**

—*Paige M.*

# I'm losing faith, slowly but surely.

—*Katheryne L.*

```
Hit and ran.
Crashed and burned.
```

—*Zoe A.*

Fourteen years old,
eight months pregnant.

—*Ashley W.*


Everything is gone
but the song.

—*Chris M.*


# Built a bridge;
# it burned down.

—*Amanda B.*


He's gay.
He's still my father.

—*Mary L.*

We're the family
you gossip about.

—*Steven M.*

**All that I need are animals.**

—*Ashley C.*


I tried to make it work.

—*Kendrah H.*


```
Former saint.
Now look at me. . . .
```
—*Siobhan C.*


# The Beatles really said it all.

—*Mary Kate C.*

I made captain, then some enemies.

—*Molly B.*

Only perfect when playing The Sims.

—*Ashleigh B.*

Drawing blanks,
    shooting blanks,
        filling blanks.

—*Katie W.*

My brain's
a box of crayons.

—*Ayana M.*

I got arrested. I saved him.
—*Emily Y.*

# I miss when boys had cooties.
—*Mary Elizabeth P.*

My friends are strangers in chatrooms.
—*Stephanie S.*

Want to be good so bad.
—*Mieke R.*

I'm too afraid to be myself.

—*Marissa K.*


Planned parenthood:
saved mine, took hers.

—*Emma L.*


Married at seventeen,
best decision ever.

—*Robin W.*


I secretly want to be androgynous.

—*Mercy P.*

Life's full of "awkward turtle" moments.

—*Anna S.*

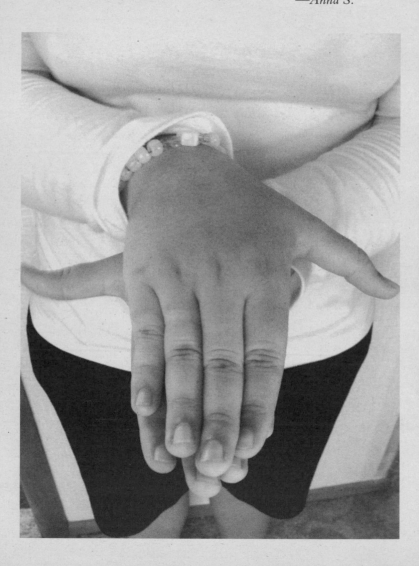

I'm waiting for my real name.

—*Joseph E.*

# Unique in high school equals freak.

—*Maryanne H.*

```
Against all odds,
I'm still myself.
```

—*Maya A.*

Some days sucked.
Sun still rose.

—*Mary H.*

I lied so you wouldn't worry.

—*Jordan S.*


## Overachieved. Love high school. Now what?

—*Meghan M.*


## Life lessons found in *Scrubs* episodes.

—*Ria H.*


`FYI: I am not my illness.`

—*Erin M.*

Chubby, but love to be naked.

—*Alyssa F.*

I'm here because of the scholarship.

—*Anna M.*

First love was worth every tear.

—*Anne K.*

Found God in bucket of paint.

—*Alex W.*

I haven't cried in seven years.

—*Megan M.*

**Called walrus.**
**Should probably feel insulted.**

—*Clara Y.*

Model and sci-fi geek.
Gotta problem?!

—*Lucy A.*

I am in a love pentagon.

—*Marissa D.*

Our love survived judgment and heartache.

—*Colleen M.*

Dreading being too busy for music.

—*Jo B.*

Coach ignored me.
He'll regret it.

—*Maeve M.*

I hate being the poor one.

—*Morgan Y.*

I pretend to be a vegetarian.

—*Liana J.*

**Momma was my life. She's gone. . . .**

—*Hannah S.*

`My boyfriend thought I liked girls.`

—*Lovelyn C.*

# Replaced Prince Charming with someone real.

—*Jessica T.*

Misunderstood,
but I'm still standing strong.

—*Mary C.*

Love sucks,
so I discovered poetry.

—*Quanesha W.*

I was named after a store.

—*Lauren B.*

My heart is in India.
Sorry.

—*Michelle K.*

Still have nightmares
of sixth grade.

—*Jackie V.*

My dad is a
compulsive hoarder.

—*Katy J.*

Tired of being the smart kid.

—*Danielle B.*

Sometimes I secretly watch
*Hannah Montana.*

—*Emily T.*

# Playground hierarchy
# was so much easier.

—*Poppy R.*


# Can't stop pulling out
# my hair.

—*Bianca B.*


**I'm poor. I'm going to Harvard.**

—*Hope P.*


Want
   to
     jump,
        afraid
            to
               fall.

—*Johannah W.*

I am a tough young broad.

—*Lacy B.*


Summer romance:
It never lasts long.

—*Kyla M.*


Always wanted
to meet Ellen DeGeneres.

—*Mackenna C.*


Don't leave me;
Daddy already did.

—*Jordan B.*

I needed Daddy;
he needed meth.
—*Alison W.*


I beat bulimia,
you can too.
—*Kristin B.*


Parents left me
at a party.
—*Lauren J.*


I was born differently—original since.
—*Vicki J.*

I miss your Swedish Fish kisses.

—*Carah N.*


`The razor never loved me back.`

—*Alyssa L.*


Half black/half Italian.
In Utah.

—*Haylee H.*


I always spell my name backwards.

—*Hannah F.*

Started
    forgetting
       about
          life
            before
               Katrina.
                    —*Grace H.*

Blessed with friends; cursed with secrets.

—*Joseph B.*

**I think in full, correct sentences.**

—*Jamille R.*

Mum's a hairdresser. I'm going university.

—*Mia W.*

My parents think it's their fault.

—*Caleb G.*

**Love:**
**not enough,**
**all there is.**

—*Katie B.*

He was the cutest stepping-stone.

—*Stephanie G.*

# Thought I was gay. Guess not.

—*Xenia P.*

Simple is desirable.
Complex is realistic.

—*Kathryn A.*

Octopus are my number One Fear.

—Benjamin M.

Lies didn't work for earning popularity.

—*Nicole M.*

I almost blew up a microwave.

—*Deanna B.*

Holden caught me in the rye.

—*Brittany F.*

Found home somewhere far from familiarity.

—*Arden B.*

Small genetic condition ruined my life.

—*Beth S.*


Strangers make me happier than friends.

—*Kara T.*


Sarcasm:
shown to those who care.

—*Paige K.*


Eventually gave up on blue hair.

—*Kelsey A.*

Afraid I'm crazy,
*Bell Jar* style.
—*Annikka T.*

415 mg of caffeine per serving.
—*Elizabeth B.*

I still read children's fiction books.
—*Jenna P.*

Lost myself in his flaring anger.
—*Asmi H.*

Frankly, I don't give a damn.

—*Karyn L.*

Insert
melodramatic
cliché-teen ick
here.

—*Jordan E.*

Shot for Ivies.
Missed.
Community College?

—*Kenzie M.*

I dislike even numbers a lot.

—*Katherine S.*

Returned home, remembered why I left.
—*Kendra L.*

# I like myself more without makeup.
—*Kelley M.*

Her touch made my scars beautiful.
—*Kelli G.*

# I want to launch a filibuster.
—*Allison H.*

Seventeenth birthday, no word from Dad.

—*Keara F.*


Becoming a psychiatrist
to understand myself.

—*Kayalee S.*


Feeling my age. Not liking it.

—*Abigail B.*


School.
Soccer.
Sweat.
Rinse.
Homework.
Repeat.

—*Kerri S.*

I giggle to cover all emotions.
—*Jessica S.*


All year prefect.
One day rebel.
—*Kirren vW.*


Once a cynic. Love changed that.
—*Kristen M.*


My short hair makes me brave.
—*Jordyn T.*

Identified more with lyrics than people.

—*Jessica S.*

My single mom raised me well.

—*Brittany R.*

Slept with a forty-year-old.

—*Jackie R.*

Show your bravery, wear silver spandex.

—*Mark W.*

Too young to decide for forever.

—*Kathleen W.*

I would have.
You never asked.

—*Kaylan L.*

Staining my clothes:
blood and chocolate.

—*Patricia G.*

I'm thankful I'm not messed up.

—*Kieran D.*

a desperate
revolutionary
without a cause

☆

—Melanie D.

Given frivolities.
Earned the good stuff.

> —*Anna M.*

## Prefer Indiana Jones to Mr. Darcy.

> —*Laura H.*

```
                    I found hope
          in clinical depression.
```

> —*Jonathan E.*

Seventeen.
Seven men.
Ten months.
Slut.

> —*Chelsea P.*

Grandma died:
nothing.
Character dies:
sobbing.
—*Anri B.*

Can I be fourteen forever,
please?
—*Emily B.*

# Now always thinking
# in six-word phrases.
—*Sarah R.*

Use makeup;
it covers the bruises.
—*Kate G.*

I don't rock;
Guitar Hero
**lies.**

—*Lacy F.*

I got help.
 It didn't help.
—*Emily G.*


Virgin is not a dirty word.
—*Erin C.*


Couldn't say it, so I sang.
—*Kenny S.*


Super powers
would make things easier.
—*Steven W.*

I'm not going to college. So?

—*Caitlin K.*


I don't believe it's on YouTube.

—*Greg A.*


I've already turned into my mother.

—*Liz F.*


My friends are dead rock stars.

—*McKenna S.*

Wanna lose virginity,
  wanna feel something.

> —*Kyle L.*

Too many colors, hair now brittle.

> —*Zoe L.*

Obama did.
  Now so can we.

> —*Calen M.*

Cold Pop-Tart;

messy hair;

running late.

> —*Kelsey H.*

The potential of the blank page.

—*Alexandria E.*

I'm shy, but not on paper.

—*Ren P.*


On Facebook. Nobody chatting with me.

—*Danielle C.*


`Sarcasm and cynicism, just a`
`facade.`

—*Maura F.*


My fiancé is Mormon.
I'm not.

—*Angela V.*

But so much has already happened. . . .

—*Luke T.*

Pencil on paper, draft after draft.

—*Rachel S.*

## But my life's only just begun.

—*Yael W.*

## My life story: to be continued.

—*Cassie H.*

_____ _____ _____

_____ _____ _____

_____

# STARS WRITE SIX-WORD MEMOIRS . . . JUST LIKE US!

**Found personal passions: storytelling and love.**

—*Ken Baumann*, The Secret Life of the American Teenager

**Didn't give up. Living my dream!**

—*Meaghan Jette Martin*, Camp Rock

**Impatient, innovative, creative, positive, humble, LEGENDARY!**

—*Orlando Brown*, That's So Raven

**Go big or go home—ironic.**

—*Daniel Magder*, Life with Derek

My diary is read by everyone.

—*Taylor Swift*


I gave my heart and soul.

—*Shawn Johnson*

Eyes closed, rain pours.
An inspiration.
—*Shailene Woodley,* The Secret Life of the American Teenager

```
All I know is I don't.
```
—*Sam Earle,* Degrassi: The Next Generation

**Never had time to look back.**
—*Jordan Hudyma,* Degrassi: The Next Generation

Nothing more expensive
than missed opportunities.
—*Argiris Karras,* Degrassi: The Next Generation

# SIX-WORD WINNERS FROM TEEN NICK

Grew up wanting to settle down.

—*Kirsten Wise*

Stepped on.
    Stepped up.
        Stepped out.

—*Kelly Skallerud*

He left. Mom cried.
Roller-coaster ride.

—*Danielle Weiler*

I'm an Etch A Sketch,
shaking.

—*Lee Weinsoff*

# SIX-WORD MEMOIRS FROM TEEN WEB STARS WE LOVE

## I did not set any limits.

*—Carl "Kidblogger" Ocab, www.carlocab.com*

Life:
random,
unpredictable,
heartbreaking, and breathtaking.

*—Ashley Qualls, www.whateverlife.com*

## Always took every opportunity I got.

*—Jesse T. Youngblood, Tooble.tv*

# INDEX